Loving

Developing acceptance of oneself and others

Carol A. Nero

Table of Contents

Get assistance

Be receptive

Be yourself

Acquire the ability to forgive

Adore yourself

Get assistance

In the same way that a mother's love for her newborn child is unconditional, romantic love, in its early stages of infatuation, can make the object of one's affection appear to be flawless. The majority of us, however, are skeptical that love without conditions, which is also fully welcoming and forgiving, can exist in our day-to-day lives. When we look in the mirror, we all see far too many imperfections and are reminded of far too many past injuries and missed opportunities to be able to love ourselves without also setting boundaries on that love.

There is a spiritual component that must be present in order for the love that you feel right now to evolve into unconditional love. As with any other spiritual objective, there is a way to achieve unconditional love, and success on this path depends on letting the process of achieving the goal take place in its own time. There are many different road maps that have been supplied by the various wisdom traditions around the world; nonetheless, I will present a few of the common aspects without any religious overlay.

First Step: Establish Communication with Your Inner Self

This entails giving oneself a higher priority in terms of self-care. You can make contact with the world that exists within you by practicing meditation, engaging in self-reflection or contemplation, and allowing yourself to be still for at least a few minutes on a daily basis. You eventually come to appreciate and take pleasure in it.

The second step is to confront your inner demons and resistance head-on.

The majority of people dislike confronting their own shortcomings and failings because they feel judged when they do so. But you are only human, and you will find that your feelings of uneasiness and anxiety represent memories from the past that may be healed. This is good news because it means that you can move on with your life. In point of fact, they want to be freed if you will just give them the opportunity to do so.

The first thing to do in the healing process is to turn within and allow the process of letting go to start. Healing can occur through a variety of different processes, including talk therapy and participation in support groups, energy work, massage, mind-body programs, and various Eastern medical treatments.

Deal with Previous Hurts as the Third Step

This is also sometimes referred to as advanced healing. You may find that as older residues of unpleasant emotions are released, you are left with resentments, hurts, and scars that need to be dealt with. This may take some time. Under the scar, such wounds have the sensation of being quite fresh. Going into these dark regions requires assistance from another person who understands the circumstance; this might be a close friend, mentor, confidante, priest, or therapist. Going into these dark places requires assistance from another person who understands the situation. My gut tells me that no one can complete this task on their own, but it does not mean that I am highlighting any sense of peril or fear. Once you get started, there is a wonderful sense of thrill and even a sense of victory in the process, even if the work may be done risk-free and without tension. Find someone who has been there before and made it through successfully and who can empathize with you completely. That's all you need to do.

Step 4: Make Peace with Your History

It's best not to rush into forgiving someone too quickly. It is far too simple to fool yourself into believing that you have let go of previous wounds and can forgive cruel treatment when, in reality, all you want is to run away from the discomfort you are feeling. The removal of suffering, which can only be accomplished through the process of healing, lays the groundwork for forgiveness that is both profound and long-lasting. It is necessary to begin by accepting oneself, as well as coming to terms with the fact that everyone else around you, including yourself, has been operating from their own unique degree of awareness. This can be fairly difficult to do when someone has badly injured you, but in order to entirely remove yourself from the wrongdoing, you have to first recognize that other people are confined within a reality from which they cannot escape.

Accept your current situation as it is and move on to the next step.

This is another stage that you shouldn't rush into too soon after the previous one. The burdens, memories, and scars of the past do not leave the current moment completely unaffected. Before you can glance around, breathe easily, and enjoy the moment you are in right now, you have to take care of them first. They need your attention. It is a fantastic place to start if you can catch yourself when you are having a horrible recollection and tell yourself, "I am not that person anymore." Because the reality is that you aren't at all.

Forming relationships with people who make you feel loved and appreciated is the sixth step.

The journey toward unconditional love is not intended to be traveled alone. You ought to travel it with people who mirror the love that you see in yourself as you travel. There is a good chance that, at some point, you will look around and discover that not all of your family members and friends are on the same page as your goals and objectives. You have the right to seek out others who understand the route you're taking and sympathize with it, and you are not obligated to turn these people away. It is more likely that they will appreciate you for who you are right now as well as who you desire to become.

Step 7: Put into action the kind of love you want to be shown in return.

A long time ago, around the time that I wrote a book called The Path to Love, I met a lot of people, the majority of whom were women, who were always waiting for "the one" to come along and sweep them off their feet. This was during the time that I was writing the book. But in all seriousness, the only way to find "the one" is to actually become "the one" for yourself. The law of attraction states that like attracts like, and the more you live up to your own ideal of love, the more another light will be drawn to you. I've been told that by focusing on this one factor, most people have been able to locate their soul mate.

If you commit some time each day to working on just one or two of these steps, you will discover a doable path that will lead you to more love in your life than you currently have. As soon as you start paying attention to the steps, they will proceed by themselves naturally. You were born to be absolutely loved and to be loved to the fullest extent possible. The unnatural part is the loss of that status and the unwillingness to return to it, and the natural part is the return, which means reconnecting with your true self. Since people have successfully traversed this path for centuries, my hope is that you will take heart and join the select group of individuals who have achieved such lofty goals. There has never been a better time to get started than right now.

Be receptive

Communication that is both open and honest is critical to the health of any relationship, but it is especially important in love partnerships. However, there are some people who, for one reason or another, are not always eager to discuss their sentiments with their friends, family, or even their spouse. This can be due to a variety of factors. It can be upsetting and discouraging when your significant other is guarded and resistant to opening up to you about their feelings and experiences. However, there are actions you can take to encourage them to do just that. Here are several reasons why someone could be closed off, as well as some suggestions on how to urge them to open up.

The primary reason a person could have a hard time opening up is that they do not feel emotionally safe to do so," It's possible that this is a reflection of how they feel about the connection between them. Either they do not believe the environment to be secure enough to reveal their inner world with their spouse, or they do not feel as though they have enough to put themselves in the relationship to desire to go further with their partner.

Previous negative experiences in relationships or trauma might also contribute to an individual's predisposition to withdraw emotionally from others. It's conceivable for this person to be "feeling shame surrounding their experience and believe they should 'cover' that part of themselves." Persons who come from cultures that are more collectivistic or more traditional may be less eager to talk about personal matters. As a rule, in many different cultures, men are not encouraged to talk about their feelings, and as a result, many men have learned to suppress these feelings from an early age on in their lives.

It is essential to keep in mind that individuals digest information in their own unique manner and at varying speeds; it is entirely possible that they are unable to respond to the questions you have posed because they have not posed the questions to themselves. Someone could have a hard time opening up if they haven't processed what they're averse to opening up about.

How to get someone to talk about themselves:

1. The key to success is consistency.

It is crucial to remain consistent in order to help create trust in your relationship, especially if your partner is coping with any of the issues listed above,

whether it be past relational trauma or an inability to process their own feelings. Those with stiff boundaries, who struggle with opening up, tend to require more time than the ordinary person to create trust, rapport, and emotional safety." That foundation can be helped along if you make it a point to always keep your word, call when you say you will, and other similar behaviors.
It is important to engage in active listening.

Even if someone has problems opening up to us, a fundamental need that we all share is the yearning to be acknowledged and comprehended by others. By providing your partner with the kind of secure environment they require, active listening is an excellent method to reassure them that you will always be there for them. "Empathy is the single most essential aspect of practicing active listening: A verbal admission of one's feelings, free from criticism or condemnation. You can do this by saying something like, "It sounds like you're feeling [insert the appropriate feeling] because [reason they might be feeling that way]," which opens the door for them to provide their perspective on the situation.

3. Ask questions...but try not to overwhelm people with them.

It is also important to find a balance between asking sensitive questions and being overly nosy, as the latter might cause your partner to draw away even further. Nobody likes to feel like they are the center of attention or the focus of others' attention, but we all want to believe that we are important and that others care about us. Too many questions can leave them feeling questioned and criticized and put them on the defensive. Be patient, and when you ask a question, don't forget to listen carefully to the response you receive.

4. Show that you are willing to share and be open with others.

Self-disclosure can also be beneficial in helping someone open up," but it must be done in a way that avoids "hijacking the conversation and making it about you." Structuring sharing and self-disclosure statements in a way that encourages the other person to express their perspective and share their experiences. Take, for instance: "I've been having a lot of trouble with social withdrawal, and as a result, I've been feeling quite lonely and frightened. How have you been doing?" It will be less likely for them to feel disregarded or silenced if you include them in your own moments of vulnerability.

5. Focus on your nonverbal cues.

Even though it may sound obvious, the importance of nonverbal clues in communication cannot be overstated. Because we have all had the experience of having the impression that someone was not speaking what they meant based on their body language, being aware of the clues that we are giving off will help to develop trust and a sense of being safe. Eye contact, facial expressions that are sincere and pleasant, and the tone of your voice are some of the things that are important to keep in mind.

Give them the impression that you cherish your relationship with them, and ask them what they require to feel secure.

If nothing else works, you might have to just come out and ask your spouse what it is they require. "This one isn't always acceptable," but if you've tried everything and are still feeling like they're shutting you out, you may say something like, 'I genuinely care about you and want to continue growing our relationship.'" It has come to my attention that every time we bring up, you immediately change the subject. I completely understand if you do not wish to discuss it, and I won't inquire further about it; nevertheless, I would like to be here for you if and when you are ready to do so. Is there anything else I can do to make you feel more comfortable sharing?"

7. Recognize the things that you want for yourself.

Last but not least, it emphasizes that it is of equal importance to acknowledge our own urge to deepen relationships more quickly than others may want to do so. It's possible that our boundaries and timelines are different or that we're each unconsciously coping with issues related to abandonment. "Reflect on your own requirements for 'knowledge' or intimacy, and realize that there might be a need to practice patience with the process" is some advice that might be helpful if you are having trouble dealing with a partner who is unwilling to open up to you.

Be yourself

Some people go through their whole lives without ever questioning or trying to comprehend who they really are. They allow others to define who they are for them. They let society decide what their objectives and aspirations should be. It is the path of least resistance.

You're not like those other people at all. You have this burning need to get to the bottom of things and figure out how to be your authentic self. When you do so, you will find that your life is replete with opportunities and satisfaction.

1. KNOW YOURSELF

Our earliest memories shape the ideas we have about ourselves and who we are. We are like sponges from birth, and throughout our lives, we continue to take in information from our surroundings without even recognizing it. When we think about ourselves, we construct an opinion that we believe to be accurate, but in reality, it is how other people want us to be. These opinions eventually turn into limiting ideas for us, and in order to find an answer to the question "How can I be myself?" you have to first remove these beliefs from your mind. The real you is hiding behind the surface.

2. REFUSE TO CONTINUE TO TALK TO YOURSELF NEGATIVELY.

Negative self-talk is the outward manifestation of limiting thoughts. Listening to your inner monologue can help you break through self-limiting ideas and figure out how to begin being yourself. It's possible that you've told yourself things like, "I've always been like this," or "I'm just not good at this." Perhaps you have convinced yourself that in order to be deserving of love, you need to be perfect. Become aware of this internal monologue and challenge it. Is it preventing people from seeing the real you?

3. FOCUS ON YOUR STRENGTHS

Your less admirable qualities do not define who you are. Change your negative beliefs about yourself into positive ones that encourage you to be who you are. When you concentrate on the positive aspects of yourself, rather than picking yourself apart, you end up building yourself up. You have no idea what your best qualities are, do you? Think back on the occasions in your life when you most felt like you were "living your best life" and "in your element." You experienced those emotions as a result of the fact that you were finally learning how to start being yourself.

4. GET OUT OF THE PAST AND INTO THE PRESENT!

Your history does not equal your future. Everyone has made errors. They do not have the right to determine who you are, and you do not owe it to them to spend the rest of your life making amends. Learn how to let go of feelings of guilt and stop living in the past by attending this lesson. Your life may be anything you want it to be, so make it special. Your life can be anything you want it to be.

How can I be true to who I am?

5. STOP CARING ABOUT WHAT THE OPINIONS OF OTHER PEOPLE ARE.

It is easier for many of us to say we don't care what other people think than it is to actually practice it. The desire to be accepted by one's peers is innate to the human condition; however, the fear of the opinions of others impedes our progress. Keep in mind that the thoughts other people have about you are really a reflection of them, not of you. You have no power to influence the thoughts and beliefs of other people. You have no choice but to get comfortable with who you are and learn how to be content with that.

6. BE OPEN TO CHANGE

The human brain is quite intricate. Our personalities are the sum total of the hundreds of events and pieces of information that are processed by our brains on a daily basis. When we consider that the brain is always adapting and learning new things, how can we expect ourselves to remain static? Realize that it is possible to modify your beliefs and tastes while still maintaining a core understanding of who you are as a person. To truly be yourself, you have to accept the fact that you will evolve over time.

7. BE VULNERABLE

It is not difficult to highlight the positive aspects of one's character. However, in order to be yourself, you must be your complete self. That entails being open to the possibility of getting hurt. The answer to the question "How can I be myself?" is to step into your pain and face your anxieties head-on. If you are asking yourself this question, the answer is to face your fears head-on. Maintain a transparent and truthful relationship with both your partner and your pals. Communicate to them how you truly feel. Share your greatest worries. It's possible that you'll be shocked by how much it improves your relationships.

8. EXPRESS YOURSELF

You can learn more about what you enjoy, how your experiences affect you, and how to start being yourself if you express yourself and let those discoveries guide you. Keep a notebook in which you record the things you did well and enjoyed each day, as well as the things you could have done better and what you could have appreciated more. Create something artistic, write a song, listen to music, or even go out and tend a garden to express yourself. When we're doing activities that we enjoy, that's when we're the most in touch with who we are.

9. Get out of your comfort zone and try something new.

Certainty is one of the Six Human Needs, and people have a strong desire for it. However, we also require expansion and variety. Tony informs us that "All progress begins at the end of your comfort zone," and this is something that we should always remember. There, too, is where the path of discovering how to be oneself for the first time begins. Try new things and pay attention to how you respond to them emotionally. When you force yourself out of your comfort zone, you'll discover things about yourself that you never imagined were possible.

10. FIND YOUR COMMUNITY

You have completed the job required on the inside. It is time to start looking for people who will support and accept the new you. When you surround yourself with the proper people, they'll bring out the best in you and help you grow rather than dragging you down or preventing you from achieving your goals. You'll finally feel like you can stop searching for how to be yourself because you'll be in a place where everyone already knows who you really are and loves you for it. When you get to this place, you'll finally feel like you can finally stop seeking how to be yourself.

Acquire the ability to forgive

Holding on to unfavorable situations increases your stress level and usually diminishes your enjoyment of life. It causes one to have feelings of resentment, anger, and upset as a result. It is essential that you have the ability to adjust, learn from your mistakes, and develop as a result of unfavorable experiences. One of the most important aspects of being able to accomplish this is the capacity to forgive oneself for any errors or transgressions that one may have committed in the past.

What is the difference between self-compassion and self-forgiveness?

Self-compassion and self-forgiveness are frequently confused with one another. Self-forgiveness is distinct from but related to, the practice of self-compassion. The following are the three defining characteristics of self-compassion:

Kindness toward oneself is essential. Because of this, it is unreasonable to expect anyone to be flawless. People who regularly engage in self-compassion remind themselves of this fact whenever the going gets rough or when things don't go according to plan. They are compassionate and loving toward themselves, and they recognize the inevitable nature of human imperfection.

The same human condition. In life, nobody escapes unscathed from difficulties. As unforeseen events unfold, everyone will go through challenging feelings and be forced to find solutions to difficult problems. Giving yourself compassion entails recognizing that you are not the only person in the world who goes through these things and letting go of the idea that you are the only one.

Clarity and attention to the present moment People often report feeling uneasy while they are experiencing unfavorable feelings. They will frequently either overstate or understate the intensity of these feelings. A sign of self-compassion is when one is able to calmly and deliberately sit with difficult feelings and recognize them for what they are.

Self-compassion is different from self-forgiveness in the sense that self-forgiveness is a way of reconciling the way you see yourself after having negative emotions such as guilt, humiliation, and disappointment. Self-compassion is a way of showing kindness and understanding to oneself.

When you do anything that calls into question the image you have of yourself, you may experience the sentiments described above. As a result, it is a component of having compassion for oneself.

Strategies for Self-Forgiveness

It's possible that you'll occasionally engage in behavior that tests how you see yourself. When someone does something that has a detrimental impact on themselves or on others, it can be challenging to make amends with themselves. Internally practicing self-forgiveness can be difficult, but here are some helpful hints:

Remember the past. Recall a time in your life when you were worried about someone you cared about, and you felt safe. Don't forget who it was; it may be a close friend or relative, a teacher or mentor, a spiritual figure, a pet, or even a spiritual guide. Imagine yourself surrounded by them and feeling safe and secure. Visualize that sensation. Let yourself feel safe. The next step is to compile a list of all of your redeeming traits with the help of your defender.

Keep the event in your mind. The next step is to admit the truth about the things you have done that you need to forgive yourself for. Think back to the particular occurrence and how it made you feel after it happened. Take note of the challenges you currently encounter. Create a list of everything that transpired and divide the items on the list into three distinct categories: ethical failings, incompetence, and everything else. Unskillfulness necessitates rectification, such as making a promise never to do a given act again, whereas moral failings ask for feelings of regret or remorse to be experienced.

Don't avoid guilt. It is good and reasonable to experience negative emotions after engaging in harmful behavior. What are we left with if we remove the negative emotions associated with doing something wrong? There is a distinction to be made between feelings of shame and those of guilt. Shame is accompanied by a variety of defensive emotions, including denial, avoidance, and even violence. It is counterproductive to have the attitude that you are an intrinsically evil person and to feel sorry about it. If you do this, you may convince yourself that you are unable to change. However, being aware of the wrongdoing you've done can make it easier to avoid doing it again.

Accept your share of the blame. You will never be able to forgive yourself if you refuse to accept responsibility for the harm you caused, not only to yourself but also to the other person. Tell them that you accept responsibility for what you've done, and make sure that you tell yourself the same thing.

Acquire the ability to totally embrace the fact that you are responsible for anything you did.

Make an effort to fix the damage. If you believe that you haven't done everything you should have in order to make amends, it may be difficult for you to truly forgive yourself for your actions. It's possible that this entails making a financial contribution, correcting some damage, or simply apologizing to another person.

Exhibit compassion for more people than just yourself. It has been discovered that people have a harder time forgiving themselves when they are also able to empathize with the other person involved in the conflict. It is natural for people to experience difficulty coping with this strain. Self-forgiveness, on the other hand, can be rendered meaningless and pointless in the absence of an empathic understanding of both oneself and the other person.

The implementation of these suggestions is challenging, but so is practicing genuine self-forgiveness. There is a good chance that this will be a very long journey that will include both low points and high points. It's possible that the unpleasant feelings you have will never leave you completely. Self-forgiveness does not have to be an act of self-indulgence; rather, it should consist of an honest assessment of your capacity for both bad and good deeds.

Adore yourself

1. Stop judging your abilities based on those of others.

We are socialized to be competitive, and as a result, it is normal for us to compare ourselves to others. But doing so puts you in harm's way. Because there is only one person who is you, there is no use in making comparisons between yourself and anyone else on the earth. Instead, make sure that you are concentrating on yourself and your trip. Simply shifting your energy will help you feel more at ease and more liberated.

2. Do not be concerned with the views of other people.

Along the same line, you shouldn't care about what other people think of you, or the expectations society has of you. Because you can't make everyone happy, wasting your time on something like this is pointless and will only serve to slow you back on your road to being the best version of yourself.

3. Give yourself permission to make errors.

Since we were very young, we have heard over and over that "nobody's perfect" and that "everyone makes errors." However, the more your age, the greater the pressure you feel to succeed at all you do. Give yourself a break and relax! Allow yourself to err in order to learn and improve from your experiences. Embrace your past. Who you were in the past gives way to who you are now and who you will become in the future; you are always evolving and developing into a better version of yourself.

Put to rest the voice in your head that tells you that you must always strive for perfection. Make a ton of mistakes; it's the only way to learn. The lessons you'll receive are priceless.

4. Remind yourself that your worth is not determined by the way your body appears.

This is of the utmost importance! There are a great number of things in our world that are actively working to divert your attention from this significant reality. There are occasions when your own internalized sexism will confirm the beliefs that you have about your inadequacy. You are valuable not because of your body but because of who you are as a person.

Therefore, you should dress in a way that makes you happy. Wear whatever it is that gives you the most self-assurance, the most comfort, and the most joy, no matter how much or how little there is.

5. You shouldn't be scared to cut ties with people that are toxic to you.

There are some people who don't believe they should be held accountable for the energy they put out into the world. If there is someone who is bringing negativity into your life and they are unable to accept responsibility for it, this may indicate that you need to distance yourself from that person. Do not let your fear stop you from doing this. Even though it could be uncomfortable, going through it is necessary and crucial.

Keep in mind that you need to guard your energy. It is neither impolite nor inappropriate to remove oneself from circumstances or the presence of people who are emotionally draining.

6. Work through your fears.

Fear is a normal and human emotion, just like making mistakes. Instead of trying to escape your concerns, try to comprehend them. This physically beneficial activity can be of great assistance in improving your mental wellness. You can acquire insight and uncover issues in your life that were giving you worry by questioning and analyzing your anxieties. This will help you overcome anxiety. That, in turn, can help ease some of — if not all of — the worry that you are feeling.

7. Have faith in your own ability to make sound choices for yourself.

We have a terrible habit of second-guessing ourselves and our capacity to act morally, despite the fact that the vast majority of the time, we actually do know in our hearts what is most beneficial. Keep in mind that the way you feel is perfectly normal. You are not becoming more detached from the world around you. You are the only person who knows you better than anyone else, so you should be your own best advocate.

8. Seize each and every chance that life puts in front of you, or make your own.

There will never be a point in your life when the time is quite right for the next significant step. Even though the circumstances may not be ideal, you shouldn't let that stop you from working toward realizing your ambitions and goals. Instead, you should make the most of this opportunity because it might never come up again.

9. Make yourself your top priority.

Don't beat yourself up over having done this. Women, in particular, are more likely to develop a habit of putting the needs of others before their own. Even while there is a right moment and a proper setting for this, you shouldn't make it a habit that compromises your mental or emotional health.
Find some time for yourself to relax and unwind. You can put a significant amount of strain on yourself if you don't take the time to decompress and recharge. Find something that helps you decompress, whether it's staying in bed all day or going outside into nature, and make time to do that thing.

10. To the fullest extent possible, feel both the joy and the anguish.

Permit yourself to experience everything to the fullest. Lean into the discomfort, find joy in the good times, and don't put any boundaries on how you feel. You can learn more about yourself and ultimately come to terms with the fact that you are not the sum total of your feelings by experiencing emotions such as fear, pain, and joy.

11. Demonstrate courage when you are in public.

You should make it a practice to say what's on your mind. The more you put your confidence through its paces, the stronger it will get. Don't bother waiting to be invited to sit down at the table; just go ahead and do it. Participate in the discussion. Please share any thoughts you have. Take action, and keep in mind that your voice carries the same weight as the voices of anybody else.

12. Learn to find beauty in the uncomplicated things

Every day, make it a point to look around you and pick out at least one object that is charming and unassuming. Take note of it, and express gratitude that it has occurred. Not only does gratitude help you gain perspective, but it's also a crucial tool for locating joy in your life.

13. Have compassion for yourself.
The world is already filled with harsh words and criticism; there's no need for you to add to it. Be friendly and encouraging to yourself, and avoid calling yourself derogatory names. Honor and rejoice in yourself. You've gone a long way and matured a lot over the years. Remember to throw a

party for yourself on a regular basis, and not just on your birthday!